Staying Human in Disaster Work

Staying Human in Disaster Work

A Field Guide to Moral Injury for Responders

G. C. SMITH

RESOURCE *Publications* • Eugene, Oregon

STAYING HUMAN IN DISASTER WORK
A Field Guide to Moral Injury for Responders

Resource Publications
An Imprint of Wipf and Stock Publishers
199 W. 8th Ave., Suite 3
Eugene, OR 97401

www.wipfandstock.com

PAPERBACK ISBN: 979-8-3852-8254-8
HARDCOVER ISBN: 979-8-3852-8255-5
EBOOK ISBN: 979-8-3852-8256-2

VERSION NUMBER 05/04/26

DISCLAIMER

This book is intended for educational and informational purposes only. It is not a substitute for professional mental health care, medical advice, or clinical treatment. Readers experiencing acute distress are encouraged to seek support from a qualified professional.

Contents

Introduction

Why This Guide Exists

People train for disaster response because they want to help.

They learn how to move quickly when something terrible has happened. They learn how to organize teams, set up shelters, distribute supplies, assess damage, and coordinate with other agencies. The training focuses on practical skills—how to work efficiently, how to stay safe, how to help communities stabilize in the chaotic hours and days after catastrophe.

All of that training matters. Lives depend on it.

But there is another part of disaster work that training rarely prepares responders for.

It is the moral weight of the work.

Many responders discover this part of the job only after they have already stepped into a disaster. They show up ready to help, and they do help. Yet somewhere in the middle of the response—or sometimes after the deployment ends—they realize that certain moments stay with them.

A conversation with a survivor keeps returning to their mind.

A decision they had to make under pressure continues to replay.

A family they could not help immediately remains vivid in memory.

Responders sometimes describe these experiences in quiet ways. They may say something like, "That moment still bothers me," or "I keep thinking about that family," or "I wish we could have done more."

These reactions are not unusual. In fact, they are one of the most common experiences in disaster response. Yet many responders assume they are alone in feeling them.

This guide exists because those experiences deserve to be named and understood.

Disaster work places responders in situations where the needs are enormous and the resources are limited. Even the best response systems cannot meet every need immediately. Responders know this intellectually, yet they often feel a deep personal responsibility for the people standing in front of them.

That responsibility is part of what makes responders good at their work. Compassion motivates people to show up when others are suffering. But compassion can also create a moral tension when responders encounter the limits of what they can do.

At certain moments in disaster work, responders realize that helping everyone is impossible.

Supplies run out.

Shelters reach capacity.

Medical teams must triage.

Recovery funds are limited.

The work reaches its limits, and responders must continue forward anyway.

These moments can create a quiet but powerful inner conflict. A responder may know that they followed the procedures correctly and did everything the situation allowed. Yet something about the moment still feels unsettled.

Psychologists and ethicists have begun using a phrase to describe experiences like this: moral injury.

Moral injury occurs when a person encounters events that challenge their deepest expectations about what is right, fair, or humane. It is not the same thing as fear or trauma. Instead, it involves a sense that something about the moral structure of the situation has been disrupted.

For disaster responders, moral injury often appears in simple but persistent questions:

Did we leave someone behind?

Why did the system fail that family?

Could I have done more?

These questions do not arise because responders lack skill or dedication. They arise because responders care deeply about the people they serve. When compassionate people encounter situations where compassion alone cannot solve the problem, the experience can leave a lasting moral impression.

Many responders carry these moments quietly. They return home, move on to the next assignment, and continue helping others. Yet certain experiences remain in the background, shaping how they think about their work and about the world.

One of the most important things responders can learn is that these reactions are not signs of weakness.

They are signs of moral awareness.

Responders notice when something about a situation feels unjust or unresolved because they care about human dignity. The same moral sensitivity that motivates people to serve others can also make them vulnerable to carrying the weight of difficult moments.

This guide was written to help responders understand those experiences and talk about them more openly.

It is not a psychological treatment manual. It is not a theological argument. And it is not a set of rules for how responders should feel after a disaster.

Instead, this guide is a field companion for the moments when the work becomes morally difficult.

Inside these pages you will find descriptions of situations that many responders recognize immediately. You will see questions that responders often ask themselves after a deployment. You will also find practices that help responders talk through these experiences with colleagues and reconnect with the deeper meaning of their work.

The goal of this guide is not to remove the moral weight of disaster work. That weight exists because the work itself is serious and important. Responders stand in places where people's lives have been disrupted, sometimes in ways that cannot be fully repaired.

But responders do not have to carry those experiences alone or in silence.

One of the strongest protections against moral injury is simple conversation. When responders share their stories with others who understand the work, the moral weight becomes easier to bear. Experiences that once felt isolating become part of a shared understanding of what the work asks of those who do it.

Disaster response is ultimately about restoring human dignity in moments when that dignity has been threatened by catastrophe. Responders help people regain safety, stability, and hope after events that have shaken their lives.

Yet responders also deserve care for their own moral and emotional well-being.

If you have ever left a disaster scene with a moment you cannot quite forget—if a certain decision, conversation, or memory still lingers—this guide was written for you.

It is meant to help you recognize that those moments are part of the work, to give language to experiences that many responders share, and to offer ways of staying human while doing work that often unfolds at the very edge of human suffering.

The work matters.

And the people who do the work matter too.

Chapter 1

The Moral Weight of Disaster Work

Most people enter disaster response because they want to help.

Some are emergency managers responsible for coordinating resources when catastrophe strikes. Some are volunteers who want to serve communities in crisis. Others are chaplains, counselors, or medical personnel who provide care to people whose lives have been suddenly disrupted.

Whatever the role, the motivation is usually the same: when something terrible happens, responders want to be part of helping people recover.

For many responders, that motivation is deeply personal. They believe that when disaster strikes, showing up for others is the right thing to do. Compassion, service, and responsibility form the moral foundation of disaster work.

This sense of purpose is one of the strongest forces in the responder community. It is why people deploy long hours, work in difficult environments, and return again and again to places where suffering is visible.

But there is another truth about disaster work that responders often discover only after they have been in the field.

Helping people in catastrophe carries a moral weight that few training programs prepare responders to recognize.

Disasters create situations where the needs are overwhelming. Homes are destroyed. Families are displaced. Entire communities struggle to regain stability. Even large response systems must work within limits of time, resources, and personnel.

At some point during most disaster responses, responders encounter those limits.

A supply truck runs out before every family receives assistance.

A shelter reaches capacity.

A medical team must prioritize who receives immediate care.

Recovery funds cannot cover every damaged home.

These situations are not failures of compassion. They are realities of disaster response. No system can eliminate all suffering in the immediate aftermath of catastrophe.

Yet for the responder standing in front of a person who needs help, those limits can feel deeply personal.

Responders often experience a moment when they realize that doing everything possible still does not mean doing enough. They must explain that help will come later, or that resources are not yet available, or that another team must handle the request.

These moments are often brief. The work continues. Other people need assistance. The responder moves on to the next task.

But sometimes the memory of that interaction remains.

Responders may find themselves replaying the moment afterward. They remember the look on someone's face, or the tone of a conversation, or the quiet disappointment when help could not be given immediately.

These memories do not appear because responders did something wrong.

They appear because responders care deeply about the people they serve.

In fact, the very qualities that make someone a good responder—compassion, responsibility, and moral commitment—also make them sensitive to situations where those values encounter limits.

This is where the moral weight of disaster work becomes visible.

Responders are not simply performing technical tasks. They are standing at the intersection of human suffering and human compassion. They are witnessing moments when people's lives have been disrupted in ways that cannot always be quickly repaired.

That experience can leave a lasting impression.

Some responders describe it as a sense that something about the situation remains unresolved. They know that the response system did everything it could within its constraints. Yet emotionally, the moment still feels unfinished.

This reaction is not unusual.

In fact, it is often a sign that the responder's moral compass is working exactly as it should.

Responders notice when a situation feels unjust or incomplete because they believe deeply in human dignity. They want people to be safe, cared for, and treated fairly. When disaster disrupts those expectations, the responder feels the tension between what should be and what is possible in the moment.

Recognizing this tension is the first step toward understanding the moral dimension of disaster work.

The purpose of this guide is not to eliminate that tension. Disaster response will always involve difficult moments and imperfect outcomes. Instead, the goal is to help responders understand why these experiences affect them and how they can talk about them with others who share the work.

When responders learn that these moments are common and understandable, something important happens. The experiences that once felt isolating become part of a shared conversation about what the work asks of those who do it.

Disaster response will always require courage, skill, and compassion.

But it also requires honesty about the moral weight responders sometimes carry.

Naming that weight is the beginning of learning how to carry it together.

FIELD REFLECTION

Think about a disaster response you have participated in.

Was there a moment when you felt the limits of what the response system could do?

What part of that moment stayed with you afterward?

CONVERSATION STARTER FOR TEAMS

After a deployment, teams can ask one simple question:

"Was there a moment during this response that felt morally difficult?"

Listening to each other's stories can help responders recognize that these experiences are shared across the team.

Chapter 2

When You Cannot Help Everyone

Sooner or later, every disaster responder encounters the same moment.

It is the moment when the need in front of you is greater than the help you can give.

Sometimes the moment comes quietly. A line of people stretches longer than the supplies available. A shelter reaches capacity while families are still arriving. A recovery program closes applications while there are still damaged homes in the community.

Other times the moment arrives suddenly. A medical team must triage patients during a crisis. A response team must move on to the next location while people are still asking for assistance.

Whatever form it takes, the realization is the same.

You cannot help everyone.

Most responders understand this reality intellectually. Disaster training teaches that resources are always limited. Response systems must prioritize. Teams must work within the constraints of time, supplies, and personnel.

Yet when responders stand face to face with someone who needs help, the experience can feel very different from the lessons learned in training.

Responders do not enter disaster work thinking about scarcity. They enter because they want to help people who are hurting. Compassion and responsibility drive them into the field.

So when a moment arrives where help cannot be given immediately—or cannot be given at all—it can leave a powerful impression.

Responders sometimes remember these moments long after the disaster itself fades from public attention.

They remember the family who came to the supply distribution after the truck was already empty.

They remember the elderly resident who could not yet receive rebuilding assistance because the program had not opened.

They remember the conversation where they had to say, "I'm sorry, but we don't have that resource available right now."

Often the responder continues working immediately afterward. There are other people waiting. The response operation must continue moving.

But later, sometimes days or weeks after the deployment, that moment may return unexpectedly.

A responder may replay the conversation in their mind.

They may wonder whether they explained the situation clearly enough. They may think about what the family experienced after they left. They may imagine what it would have felt like to be on the other side of the conversation.

None of these reflections mean the responder made a mistake.

In most cases, the responder handled the situation exactly as they were trained to do. The limits of the response system were real. No individual responder had the power to change those limits.

Yet the moment still carries weight.

That weight often appears as a quiet question that lingers beneath the surface of the responder's memory:

Did we leave someone behind?

This question is not a failure of professionalism. It is a sign of moral awareness. The responder recognizes the gap between what compassion hopes to accomplish and what the situation allowed in that moment.

Disasters often create that gap.

The scale of destruction may exceed the resources available in the first days or weeks of response. Programs designed to help survivors must establish rules that determine eligibility. Recovery systems sometimes move slowly while communities need help immediately.

Responders frequently stand at the point where these limitations become visible to survivors.

They become the human face of a system that cannot meet every need at once.

That position can be morally difficult.

Responders care deeply about the people they serve. When someone stands in front of them asking for help, the responder wants to provide it. Having to explain that assistance will come later—or may not come at all—can feel like a personal failure even when it is not.

Understanding this dynamic is an important step toward recognizing moral injury in disaster work.

Moral injury does not arise only from dramatic or catastrophic moments. Sometimes it grows out of small encounters that carry deep moral significance.

A brief conversation.

A decision made under pressure.

A moment when compassion meets the limits of what is possible.

These experiences often stay with responders because they touch the core reason people entered disaster work in the first place. Responders want to relieve suffering. When the work prevents them from doing that fully, the tension between intention and outcome can remain unresolved.

One of the most important things responders can learn is that this tension is not theirs to carry alone.

Every disaster response system faces limits. Every responder will eventually encounter moments where the need exceeds the available resources. These situations are part of the reality of disaster work.

Talking about them openly can reduce the sense of isolation that responders sometimes feel afterward.

When responders share these experiences with colleagues, they often discover that others remember similar moments. The stories may differ in detail, but the underlying experience is familiar.

Someone remembers a family that could not receive assistance immediately.

Someone else recalls a shelter that reached capacity.

Another responder describes a difficult conversation with a survivor who was understandably frustrated.

Through these conversations responders begin to recognize that the moral weight of the work is shared.

No single responder carries responsibility for the limits of disaster response. Those limits are built into the scale and complexity of the events responders confront.

What responders can do is acknowledge these moments, learn from them, and support each other as they continue the work.

Helping people in catastrophe is one of the most meaningful forms of service a person can offer.

But meaningful work often carries emotional and moral weight.

Recognizing that weight—and sharing it with others—is one way responders remain human while continuing to serve communities in crisis.

FIELD REFLECTION

Think about a time during disaster response when someone asked for help that could not be provided immediately.

What part of that moment stayed with you?

What thoughts or questions surfaced afterward?

TEAM CONVERSATION

After a deployment, teams can discuss a question like this:

"Did anyone encounter a moment during this response where we reached the limits of what we could do?"

These conversations help responders recognize that these experiences are common and shared across the team.

Chapter 3

The Moments That Stay With You

Disaster responses eventually end.

The shelters close. The supply distribution sites pack up their tables. Response vehicles leave town. Emergency operations centers return to normal routines.

For many responders, the transition happens quickly.

One week they are working long hours in the middle of crisis. The next week they are back at their regular jobs, sitting at a desk, attending meetings, or returning to ordinary daily life.

On the surface, everything appears normal again.

But sometimes something from the deployment lingers.

It may begin with a memory that returns unexpectedly.

A conversation with a survivor comes to mind while driving home from work. A particular scene reappears while lying awake at night. A face from the response suddenly appears in memory during a quiet moment.

The responder may not understand why that particular moment remains so vivid.

It was only a small interaction in the middle of a very busy response.

But something about it refuses to fade.

Many responders experience this phenomenon at some point in their work. Certain moments from the field stay with them long after the deployment has ended.

Sometimes the memory is tied to a situation where someone was suffering deeply.

A parent searching through debris for something belonging to their child.

An elderly resident returning to a home that no longer exists.

A survivor standing silently while looking at the remains of their neighborhood.

At other times the moment that lingers involves a difficult interaction.

A conversation where the responder had to say no.

A situation where the system could not provide help immediately.

A moment when frustration or anger surfaced from someone who had lost everything.

These experiences can leave responders with a quiet sense that something about the moment remains unfinished.

The responder knows that they did their job.

They followed protocol.

They worked within the system that was in place.

And yet, emotionally, the moment still carries weight.

This reaction often surprises responders.

Most people assume that the hardest part of disaster work happens during the deployment itself. They expect long hours, difficult scenes, and intense responsibility.

What many responders do not expect is that certain moments may return later, after the work has ended.

These memories do not necessarily appear as dramatic trauma. Instead they often feel like a quiet question that continues to surface.

Could I have done more?

Did we do enough?

What happened to that family afterward?

These questions arise not because responders failed, but because responders care.

Disaster work places people in situations where compassion encounters suffering on a daily basis. The human mind naturally tries to make sense of these experiences afterward.

Sometimes that process of reflection leads responders to recognize that the work touched them more deeply than they realized in the moment.

This is where the concept of moral injury becomes important.

Moral injury occurs when someone experiences events that challenge or disrupt their deepest moral expectations. In disaster work, those expectations often involve beliefs about fairness, responsibility, and the desire to protect people from harm.

When responders encounter situations where those values cannot be fully realized, the experience can leave an emotional mark.

The responder may not feel traumatized in the traditional sense. They may not experience fear or flashbacks related to danger.

Instead they may feel something quieter but still powerful.

A sense that the world is not as morally coherent as they once believed.

A lingering sadness about what people endured.

A question about whether the response system could ever truly meet the needs created by catastrophe.

These reflections are not signs of weakness.

In fact, they are often signs of a responder who remains deeply connected to the moral purpose of their work.

Responders who care about human dignity will naturally notice when that dignity has been wounded.

They will remember the moments where the gap between what people deserve and what the situation allowed became painfully visible.

Recognizing this dynamic can be incredibly helpful for responders.

When people understand that these experiences are common in disaster work, the memories that once felt confusing begin to make more sense.

They realize that the lingering moments are not evidence that something is wrong with them.

They are evidence that they were fully present to the human realities of the disaster.

The goal of this manual is not to remove those memories.

Many responders would not want to erase them even if they could. Those memories often represent the moments when the responder's compassion was most deeply engaged.

Instead, the goal is to help responders learn how to carry those memories in a healthy way.

Talking about them.

Reflecting on them.

Recognizing that others in the field have experienced similar moments.

When responders begin to share these stories with one another, the experiences that once felt isolating become part of a shared understanding of the work.

And that shared understanding can become one of the most powerful forms of support responders have.

FIELD REFLECTION

Is there a moment from disaster response that still returns to you unexpectedly?

What part of that moment remains vivid?

What questions, if any, still surface when you think about it?

TEAM CONVERSATION

After a response, teams may ask:

"Was there a moment from this deployment that has stayed with you?"

These conversations help responders recognize that these memories are a normal part of meaningful service.

Chapter 4

Why Good Responders Are Vulnerable to Moral Injury

Most responders do not expect that the work itself might affect them morally.

When people think about the challenges of disaster response, they usually imagine physical exhaustion, long deployments, difficult logistics, or exposure to traumatic scenes. These are real pressures, and responder training often addresses them through safety protocols, rest schedules, and stress management strategies.

But there is another dimension of the work that is less visible.

Disaster response places people in situations where their deepest values are constantly engaged.

Responders care about protecting life. They care about fairness. They care about helping people recover dignity after catastrophe has disrupted their lives. These values often draw people into the field in the first place.

The responder who volunteers to deploy during a flood, tornado, or wildfire is usually someone who believes strongly that human suffering matters and that communities should not face disasters alone.

These convictions are strengths.

They are the very qualities that make disaster response possible. Without people who care deeply about the wellbeing of others, disaster response systems would not function.

Yet these same qualities can also make responders vulnerable to moral injury.

The reason is simple.

When someone is deeply committed to helping others, they notice the moments when help cannot be given.

When someone believes strongly in fairness, they feel the tension when assistance cannot reach everyone at the same time.

When someone values human dignity, they recognize the moments when disaster has stripped that dignity away.

Responders who care deeply do not ignore these moments. They absorb them.

This does not mean responders are doing something wrong. In fact, it often means they are doing their work with great integrity.

But integrity has a cost.

A responder who pays attention to the moral dimension of the work will sometimes carry the emotional weight of situations that others might overlook.

Consider two different ways someone might approach disaster response.

One responder treats the work purely as a technical assignment. They follow procedures, complete tasks, and move on to the next responsibility without reflecting much on the human stories unfolding around them.

Another responder approaches the work relationally. They listen carefully to survivors, notice the emotional impact of the disaster, and think deeply about what the experience means for the people they serve.

Both responders may perform their duties effectively.

But the second responder—the one who connects emotionally and morally with the work—is more likely to carry memories and questions afterward.

The reason is not weakness.

It is compassion.

Compassion keeps responders attentive to the suffering around them. It allows them to offer presence and care in moments when people feel vulnerable and disoriented.

Yet compassion also means that responders do not simply observe suffering from a distance.

They encounter it directly.

This is why some of the most dedicated responders sometimes struggle with the emotional aftermath of disaster work.

They remember the moments when someone needed help that was not immediately available.

They think about the families who will face a long recovery process.

They wonder about people they met briefly but whose lives were deeply disrupted.

None of these reflections mean the responder did something wrong.

They mean the responder was paying attention.

Understanding this truth can be deeply reassuring for people in disaster work.

Many responders assume that if they feel affected by the work, it must mean they are not strong enough or experienced enough. They may compare themselves to colleagues who appear unaffected and wonder whether something is wrong with them.

In reality, the opposite may be true.

The responders who feel the moral weight of the work are often the ones who care the most about doing it well.

Their reactions reflect the very values that make disaster response humane.

This insight changes the way responders can think about moral injury.

Instead of seeing it as a problem to be hidden or avoided, responders can recognize it as a signal that their moral awareness is active.

It shows that they remain connected to the reason they entered disaster work in the first place.

The goal, then, is not to eliminate compassion or moral awareness.

Those qualities are essential.

The goal is to learn how to carry the moral weight of the work without carrying it alone.

Responders who talk openly with colleagues about the difficult moments they encounter often discover that others have experienced the same tensions.

They hear stories that echo their own experiences.

They realize that the questions they have asked themselves are questions others have asked as well.

This shared recognition can transform how responders experience the work.

Instead of feeling isolated in their reflections, they begin to understand that the moral dimension of disaster response is something the entire responder community navigates together.

Disaster response will always involve difficult moments.

No training program can remove the reality that human suffering accompanies disasters. Responders will continue to encounter situations where compassion meets the limits of what is possible.

But when responders understand why these moments affect them, the experience becomes easier to process.

They recognize that the moral weight they feel is not a burden they created.

It is part of the work itself.

And the fact that they feel it may be one of the clearest signs that they remain fully human while doing extraordinarily difficult work.

FIELD REFLECTION

Think about the values that first drew you into disaster response.

What beliefs about helping others motivated you to serve?

How do those values shape the way you experience difficult moments in the field?

TEAM CONVERSATION

Response teams can explore this question together:

"What values brought us into this work in the first place?"

Remembering those motivations can help responders understand why the work sometimes affects them so deeply—and why those reactions are often signs of compassion rather than weakness.

Chapter 5

What Moral Injury Actually Is

The phrase moral injury can sound intimidating at first.

Many responders hear the term and assume it refers to something severe or clinical. They may imagine it applies only to soldiers returning from war or to people who have experienced extreme psychological trauma.

But the basic idea behind moral injury is much simpler.

Moral injury occurs when someone experiences a situation that deeply conflicts with their sense of what is right.

That conflict can appear in many different ways.

Sometimes it happens when a person feels responsible for something that went wrong.

Sometimes it happens when someone witnesses injustice or suffering that should not have happened.

Sometimes it occurs when a person is placed in a situation where every available option feels morally incomplete.

In disaster response, moral injury often arises in moments when responders encounter the limits of what the system can do.

A responder may stand in front of someone who needs help and realize that the help cannot be provided immediately.

A team may have to make difficult decisions about how to distribute limited resources.

A responder may witness suffering that no amount of effort can quickly repair.

None of these situations mean the responder has done something wrong.

In fact, most of the time responders are doing exactly what the system requires and exactly what the situation allows.

Yet the experience can still leave a mark.

The reason is that disaster work constantly engages the responder's moral values.

Responders believe people should be safe.

They believe families should not lose everything in a moment.

They believe communities deserve dignity and support during recovery.

When disasters disrupt those expectations, responders experience the same tension survivors feel: the world suddenly seems less fair than it should be.

Most responders do not describe this feeling using psychological language.

Instead they say things like:

"That moment stayed with me."

"Something about that situation never felt right."

"I still think about that family sometimes."

These reactions are common in people who do work rooted in compassion.

Doctors, firefighters, humanitarian workers, and counselors often report similar experiences. Whenever someone dedicates themselves to helping others, they eventually encounter situations where the help they want to provide cannot fully meet the need.

That gap between what we hope to do and what is possible in the moment is often where moral injury lives.

One of the most important things responders can understand is that moral injury is not a sign that something is wrong with them.

It is often a sign that their moral compass is working.

People who do not care deeply about human suffering rarely struggle with these questions. The responders who notice the moral tension in disaster work are usually the ones who are paying the closest attention to the dignity of the people they serve.

In that sense, moral injury is not evidence of weakness.

It is evidence of moral awareness.

This does not mean the experience should be ignored.

When responders carry difficult memories or unresolved questions for long periods of time, the weight can gradually accumulate. Responders may begin to feel more cynical, more emotionally distant, or more exhausted by the work they once loved.

That is why naming moral injury can be helpful.

Once responders understand what the experience is, they often feel a sense of relief. The moments that once felt confusing begin to make more sense. They realize that other people in the field have experienced the same tension.

The conversation shifts from "What is wrong with me?" to "This is something that happens in this work."

That shift is powerful.

It opens the door to healthier ways of processing the experiences responders carry.

Instead of holding difficult moments privately, responders can talk about them with colleagues who understand the same realities.

Instead of interpreting their reactions as personal failure, they can recognize them as part of the moral landscape of disaster response.

And instead of withdrawing from the work they care about, they can learn how to continue serving while protecting their own humanity.

Moral injury does not mean a responder should stop caring.

It means the responder has encountered the deep moral challenges that accompany compassionate work.

Learning how to navigate those challenges is part of becoming a resilient responder.

FIELD REFLECTION

Have you ever experienced a moment in disaster work where the situation conflicted with your sense of what was right?

What about that moment stayed with you?

TEAM CONVERSATION

Ask your team this question:

"What situations in disaster work create the hardest moral tensions for responders?"

You may discover that many of the answers sound very familiar.

Chapter 6

How Moral Injury Shows Up in Responders

Moral injury rarely announces itself clearly.

Unlike physical exhaustion or operational stress, it does not always appear in ways that are immediately recognizable. Responders may complete a deployment successfully, return home, and resume their normal routines without any obvious signs that the experience affected them deeply.

But over time, small changes may begin to appear.

These changes are often subtle at first.

A responder who once spoke enthusiastically about deployments may become quieter when the topic comes up. Someone who used to volunteer quickly for new assignments may hesitate. A responder who once felt energized by helping others may begin to feel strangely detached from the work.

These reactions do not necessarily appear immediately after a disaster response. In many cases they emerge gradually, sometimes weeks or months later.

The responder may not even connect the feeling to a specific deployment.

They simply notice that something about the work feels different.

One common experience is a quiet sense of unfinished responsibility.

Responders may think about people they encountered during a disaster and wonder what happened to them afterward. They may recall families who were still waiting for assistance when the response operation ended. They may remember someone they spoke with briefly and feel a lingering sense that the story did not reach resolution.

These reflections often surface during ordinary moments—while driving, doing routine work, or lying awake at night.

Another common experience is frustration with the response system itself.

Responders understand that disaster operations require organization, rules, and prioritization. These systems are necessary for large-scale response efforts to function effectively.

Yet responders also witness the human consequences of those systems.

They see situations where bureaucratic processes move more slowly than survivors need. They encounter cases where eligibility requirements prevent assistance from reaching someone who clearly needs help. They hear stories from survivors that reveal gaps in the response structure.

Over time, some responders begin to feel tension between the system they represent and the people they serve.

They may start to ask themselves difficult questions.

Is this the best we can do?

Why does it take so long for people to receive help?

Could the system work differently?

These questions often arise from the responder's desire to see people treated fairly. But when the responder feels powerless to change the system, the frustration can linger.

Another way moral injury appears is through emotional distancing.

Responders who have encountered repeated scenes of suffering sometimes begin to protect themselves by becoming less emotionally involved. Instead of listening deeply to survivors' stories, they may focus strictly on completing tasks. Instead of engaging personally with the people they serve, they may keep conversations brief and procedural.

This distancing is not necessarily intentional.

It is often the mind's way of managing repeated exposure to difficult situations. By creating emotional space, the responder protects themselves from being overwhelmed.

Yet emotional distancing can also create its own challenges.

Many responders entered disaster work precisely because they wanted to connect with people and offer meaningful support during difficult moments. When that sense of connection begins to fade, the work may start to feel less meaningful.

Some responders describe this as a kind of numbness.

They continue doing the work competently, but the emotional engagement that once motivated them feels diminished.

A related experience is quiet guilt.

Responders may carry the sense that they should have done more, even when the situation made that impossible. They may replay certain moments from the response and imagine alternative outcomes.

These reflections rarely involve clear mistakes.

Instead they reflect the responder's desire to have protected or helped someone more fully.

Over time, these feelings can accumulate if they remain unspoken.

Responders may begin to feel more tired than usual, not only physically but emotionally. They may find themselves questioning whether the work is making the difference they once believed it did.

It is important to recognize that these reactions do not mean a responder is failing.

They are often signs that the responder has been paying close attention to the human reality of disaster.

Responders who care deeply about the people they serve naturally absorb some of the emotional and moral complexity of the work. The challenge is not to eliminate that awareness but to ensure it does not become isolating.

One of the most helpful things responders can do is recognize that these experiences are common.

When responders begin to talk openly with colleagues about the moments that stayed with them, they often discover that others have experienced similar reactions.

Someone else remembers a difficult conversation.

Someone else has questioned whether the system could have responded differently.

Someone else has felt the tension between compassion and the limits of what was possible.

These conversations can be surprisingly relieving.

The responder who once thought they were alone in their reflections suddenly realizes that the experience is shared across the responder community.

Instead of carrying the weight privately, responders can begin to process it collectively.

Understanding how moral injury appears in disaster work is an important step toward addressing it.

Once responders recognize the patterns—unfinished responsibility, frustration with the system, emotional distancing, quiet guilt—they can begin to respond to those experiences intentionally.

And most importantly, they can begin to support one another in ways that help everyone remain connected to the purpose that first brought them into the work.

FIELD REFLECTION

Have you noticed any changes in how you experience disaster response over time?

Are there moments or memories from deployments that still return unexpectedly?

TEAM CONVERSATION

Ask your team this question during a post-deployment discussion:

"How does this work stay with us after the deployment ends?"

Chapter 7

You Are Not the Only One Carrying This

One of the most difficult aspects of moral injury is how quietly it develops.

Responders rarely talk about these experiences openly. Disaster work often emphasizes strength, competence, and reliability. People depend on responders to remain calm and focused during chaotic situations.

Because of this culture, responders sometimes assume that the moral weight they feel is something they should handle privately.

They may think:

Everyone else seems fine.

Maybe I'm the only one who still thinks about these things.

I should probably just move on.

So the responder keeps the experience to themselves.

They continue doing the work. They attend the next deployment, the next training, the next planning meeting. Outwardly nothing appears different.

But internally the responder may still carry certain moments from previous responses.

A conversation with a survivor.

A difficult decision made during resource shortages.

A scene from a neighborhood where everything had been destroyed.

The responder assumes that these memories are unique to them.

Yet something surprising often happens when responders begin to talk with each other honestly.

They discover that many of their colleagues remember similar moments.

One responder may mention a family they still think about years later.

Another responder may describe the frustration of having to enforce program rules that prevented someone from receiving assistance.

A third responder may admit that certain deployments affected them more deeply than they expected.

When these conversations happen, the room often grows quiet for a moment.

Not because people are uncomfortable.

But because they suddenly recognize something important.

They are not alone.

The experiences they thought were private are actually shared across the responder community.

This realization can be profoundly relieving.

For many responders, the hardest part of moral injury is not the experience itself but the isolation that surrounds it. When people believe they are the only ones carrying these questions or memories, the weight can feel heavier.

But when responders hear others describe similar experiences, something changes.

The story becomes collective.

Instead of thinking, "Why does this still bother me?" the responder begins to think, "This must be part of the work we all do."

Disaster response places people in situations where moral complexity is unavoidable. Responders witness suffering that cannot be fully repaired. They encounter moments where compassion meets limits. They make decisions that affect real people during difficult circumstances.

It would be surprising if these experiences did not leave an impression.

The responder community often contains a quiet understanding of this reality, even if it is not always spoken directly.

Experienced responders sometimes recognize the signs in each other.

They notice when a colleague becomes unusually quiet after a difficult deployment. They see when someone needs a moment to step away from a conversation. They understand the look that passes between responders who have both witnessed the same difficult scene.

These small signals reflect a shared awareness that disaster work affects the people who do it.

One of the most important protective factors against moral injury is community.

Responders who have trusted colleagues they can speak with openly are far less likely to feel isolated in their experiences. A brief conversation with someone who understands the realities of disaster work can often provide more relief than hours of private reflection.

This does not require formal counseling or structured debriefings every time a difficult moment occurs.

Sometimes it simply means having a colleague who can listen.

Someone who understands the context of the work.

Someone who does not need a long explanation to grasp why a particular moment mattered.

These conversations remind responders that they belong to a community of people who share the same commitment to helping others.

They also reinforce an important truth.

Disaster response has always been collective work.

No single responder carries the responsibility for solving the crisis alone. The entire system—local agencies, volunteers, nonprofits, government responders, and community leaders—works together to address the needs created by disaster.

The same principle applies to the emotional and moral dimensions of the work.

Responders do not need to carry those experiences alone either.

When responders share their stories with one another, the weight becomes distributed across the community rather than resting on one individual.

This is not a sign of weakness.

It is a recognition that meaningful work often requires shared support.

The goal of disaster response has always been to help communities recover from catastrophe.

But responders themselves are also part of a community.

And communities are strongest when people are able to speak honestly about the realities they face together.

FIELD REFLECTION

Think about the colleagues you trust most in disaster work.

Who could you speak with if a deployment left you carrying difficult questions or memories?

TEAM CONVERSATION

A helpful team question after deployment:

"What part of this response affected you personally?"

Even brief conversations around this question can reduce the isolation responders sometimes feel.

Chapter 8

How Responders Begin to Repair Moral Injury

Recognizing moral injury is an important first step.

Many responders feel a sense of relief simply from discovering that the experiences they carry have a name. Understanding that moral tension is a normal part of disaster work can remove the feeling that something is personally wrong.

But recognition alone is not the whole journey.

Responders also need ways to process and repair the moral weight they carry so that the work does not slowly erode the compassion that first brought them into the field.

The good news is that responders have been doing this work of repair for a long time, even if they have not always used that language.

In disaster response communities across the country, experienced responders have developed informal practices that help people carry the emotional and moral impact of the work. These practices often emerge naturally when responders talk honestly about what they have experienced.

Over time, several patterns appear again and again.

These patterns represent the beginning of moral repair.

TELLING THE STORY

One of the most powerful ways responders begin to repair moral injury is by telling the story of what they experienced.

When a deployment ends, responders often carry vivid memories of certain moments. Yet those moments can remain fragmented in the mind when they are never spoken aloud.

Sharing the story helps place the experience into a larger narrative.

A responder might describe a difficult interaction with a survivor. Another might talk about a decision the team had to make under pressure. Someone else may recall a scene that captured the emotional impact of the disaster.

As these stories are shared, something important happens.

The experience moves from private memory into shared understanding.

Other responders may add their own perspectives, recall similar situations, or simply acknowledge that the moment was difficult.

This process helps the responder realize that the experience is part of the collective reality of the work rather than something they must interpret alone.

NAMING THE MORAL TENSION

Another important step in repair is naming the moral tension directly.

Responders often describe situations using operational language—resources were limited, procedures had to be followed, or the response moved according to protocol.

While these descriptions are accurate, they sometimes leave the moral dimension of the moment unspoken.

Naming the tension can sound simple but powerful:

"It was hard to leave when people were still waiting."

"I wish we could have helped that family sooner."

"That situation didn't feel fair."

Statements like these acknowledge that the responder noticed something morally difficult in the situation.

When these observations are spoken openly, others often nod in recognition. The room becomes a place where responders can admit that disaster work sometimes places them in situations where compassion and circumstance collide.

Naming the tension does not solve the problem immediately.

But it allows responders to face the experience honestly instead of quietly carrying it alone.

RESTORING DIGNITY

Repair also occurs when responders reconnect with the deeper purpose of their work.

Disasters disrupt people's lives in profound ways. Homes are lost, routines collapse, and communities struggle to regain stability. In these moments, even small acts of care can restore a sense of dignity.

Responders often remember moments when someone expressed gratitude after receiving help.

A survivor may thank the team for listening.

A family may express relief simply because someone showed up.

A community leader may acknowledge that the presence of responders helped people feel less alone.

These moments matter.

They remind responders that even when they cannot solve every problem, their presence still makes a difference.

Sometimes the most meaningful form of assistance is not the immediate resolution of every need but the assurance that someone is standing with people during a difficult time.

Remembering these moments helps balance the memories of situations where help was limited.

RECONNECTING WITH PURPOSE

Over time, responders who experience moral injury sometimes begin to question whether the work truly makes a difference.

Reconnecting with the larger purpose of disaster response can help restore meaning.

Responders may reflect on the broader impact of their work: communities that eventually rebuilt, families who received assistance months later, or response systems that improved because lessons were learned from previous disasters.

The work of disaster response often unfolds over long timelines. Immediate results may not always be visible during the first days or weeks of response.

But when responders step back and look at the broader picture, they often see evidence that the work contributes to recovery in ways that are not always obvious in the moment.

SHARING THE WORK

Perhaps the most important element of moral repair is remembering that disaster response has always been shared work.

No single responder carries the responsibility for solving the crisis alone. Large networks of organizations, volunteers, government agencies, and community leaders collaborate to support recovery.

The emotional and moral dimensions of the work can also be shared.

When responders talk with trusted colleagues about the moments that stayed with them, they begin to distribute the weight across the community instead of carrying it privately.

This shared processing strengthens the resilience of the responder community itself.

Instead of withdrawing from the work, responders remain connected to one another and to the values that first brought them into the field.

CONTINUING THE WORK

Repair does not mean forgetting difficult moments.

Many responders continue to remember certain scenes or conversations for years. In some cases those memories remain powerful precisely because they represent moments when the responder's compassion was fully engaged.

The goal of repair is not to erase those memories.

The goal is to integrate them into a larger understanding of the work.

When responders learn to talk about these experiences, reflect on their meaning, and support one another through the process, the memories become part of the wisdom that experienced responders carry into future deployments.

They become reminders of why the work matters.

And they strengthen the responder's commitment to serve communities with both skill and humanity.

FIELD REFLECTION

Think about a moment during disaster response that still feels unfinished.

Have you ever shared that story with another responder?

What happened when you did?

TEAM CONVERSATION

After a deployment, teams might ask:

"What story from this response do you think will stay with you?"

These conversations often become the beginning of moral repair for responders who have carried the experience privately.

Chapter 9

How Teams Can Protect Each Other

Disaster response is rarely an individual effort.

Every response operation depends on teams. Emergency managers coordinate agencies and resources. Volunteers work together to distribute supplies. Medical personnel collaborate in triage and care. Spiritual care providers support survivors while relying on colleagues for guidance and backup.

Responders depend on one another for the success of the mission.

But teams serve another important role that is sometimes less visible.

They protect each other.

When teams function well, they provide not only logistical coordination but also emotional and moral support. They create an environment where responders can do difficult work without feeling isolated in the experiences they encounter.

This kind of protection does not usually happen through formal policies alone.

It grows out of the culture of the team.

Some teams develop a culture where responders know they can speak honestly about what they are experiencing. Difficult moments from the field are discussed openly. Colleagues check in with one another after challenging interactions. Leaders acknowledge that disaster work affects the people who do it.

Other teams may unintentionally communicate a different message.

In some environments, responders feel pressure to appear unaffected by the work. Conversations remain strictly operational. Emotional or moral reflections are quietly set aside because they are perceived as distractions from the task.

When this happens, responders may still perform their duties effectively.

But they may carry the deeper weight of the work privately.

The difference between these two environments can significantly influence how responders process their experiences.

CREATING A CULTURE OF CONVERSATION

Teams that protect one another often share a simple habit: they make space for conversation.

This does not require lengthy formal debriefings after every response. Sometimes it begins with small moments of connection.

A supervisor asks a responder how they are doing after a difficult shift.

Colleagues gather briefly at the end of a long day and reflect on what they encountered.

A team leader acknowledges that certain situations during the response were emotionally challenging.

These conversations send an important message.

They signal that responders are not expected to carry their experiences alone.

When people know that honest conversation is welcome, they are more likely to share the moments that affected them before those experiences become isolating.

PAYING ATTENTION TO EACH OTHER

Responders often notice subtle changes in colleagues long before those changes are recognized by the individuals themselves.

A team member who normally engages easily may become unusually quiet.

Someone who usually volunteers for new tasks may hesitate.

Another responder may appear more irritable or withdrawn than usual.

These signals do not always indicate moral injury, but they can be signs that a responder is carrying something difficult from the field.

Experienced teams learn to pay attention to these shifts.

A simple question such as "How are you doing after today?" can open a conversation that helps a colleague process a difficult moment before it grows heavier.

Often the responder will simply need someone who understands the context of the work.

LEADERSHIP MATTERS

Team leaders play a crucial role in shaping the culture of a response team.

When leaders acknowledge that disaster work can have emotional and moral impact, they give others permission to do the same.

Leaders who occasionally share their own reflections about difficult moments demonstrate that thoughtful processing of the work is not a weakness.

Instead, it is part of responsible leadership.

At the same time, leaders must balance these conversations with the operational demands of disaster response. Teams still need to remain focused, organized, and effective.

The goal is not to shift attention away from the mission.

The goal is to ensure that the people carrying out the mission are supported as they do the work.

INFORMAL DEBRIEFING

Some teams develop simple practices that help responders process experiences together.

After a particularly intense day, a team may gather briefly and ask a few guiding questions:

What was the most difficult moment today?

What is one thing you will remember from this response?

Is there anything we need to talk about before we leave tonight?

These conversations often last only a few minutes, but they create a shared space where responders can acknowledge the human dimension of the work.

Even brief conversations can prevent responders from leaving the deployment with unspoken questions or unresolved tension.

LOOKING OUT FOR EACH OTHER

Responders often say that the most important support they receive during disaster operations comes from other responders.

People who share the same work understand the pressures, the unpredictability, and the moral complexity of disaster response in ways that outsiders may not fully grasp.

Because of this shared understanding, responders are often uniquely positioned to support one another.

A colleague who quietly listens.

A teammate who offers encouragement.

A supervisor who checks in after a difficult interaction.

These gestures may seem small, but they reinforce a powerful truth.

No responder stands alone in the work.

STRENGTHENING THE COMMUNITY

Over time, teams that practice these habits develop a strong sense of community.

Responders trust that they can rely on one another not only for operational coordination but also for personal support. Difficult moments are acknowledged rather than ignored. Successes are celebrated together. Lessons from each response are shared openly.

This kind of environment strengthens both the effectiveness and the resilience of the response team.

Responders remain engaged with the work because they know that their colleagues understand the realities they face.

And when moralinjury does arise—as it inevitably will in some form—the responder already has a community ready to help carry the weight.

FIELD REFLECTION

Think about a response team you have been part of that felt particularly supportive.

What did that team do that helped people feel safe talking about difficult moments?

TEAM CONVERSATION

Ask this question during a training or team meeting:

"What can we do as a team to make sure no one carries the difficult parts of this work alone?"

The answers to this question often become the foundation of a healthy responder culture.

Chapter 10

The Role of Meaning and Purpose in Disaster Response

One of the strongest protections responders have against moral injury is something that existed long before they ever deployed to a disaster.

It is the reason they chose to serve in the first place.

Most responders do not enter disaster work by accident. Something in their life history led them toward helping others during crisis. For some it is a professional calling. For others it grows out of personal values, community commitment, or faith.

Whatever the source, responders often carry a strong sense of purpose.

They believe that when disaster strikes, someone should show up.

They believe that communities should not face catastrophe alone.

They believe that people deserve dignity and support during the hardest moments of their lives.

These convictions give disaster response its moral foundation.

Yet during difficult deployments, responders sometimes lose sight of that foundation. The scale of destruction may feel overwhelming. Recovery may move more slowly than survivors hope. Responders may encounter frustration, grief, or anger from people whose lives have been disrupted.

In these moments the work can begin to feel heavy.

Responders may find themselves asking quiet questions:

Does this really make a difference?

Are we doing enough to help people recover?

Why does the system move so slowly when people need help right now?

These questions are natural responses to the complexity of disaster response. They reflect the responder's desire to see real progress in the lives of the people they serve.

But when responders remain inside these questions without reconnecting to the larger meaning of their work, the sense of purpose that once sustained them can begin to fade.

Reconnecting with purpose is an important part of moral repair.

THE VALUE OF SHOWING UP

One of the most meaningful things responders provide during disasters is something that rarely appears in official reports.

They show up.

When communities experience catastrophe, the first days and weeks often feel chaotic and uncertain. Survivors may feel abandoned, overwhelmed, or unsure how recovery will even begin.

The presence of responders changes that experience.

When emergency managers coordinate response efforts, when volunteers distribute supplies, when counselors listen to survivors' stories, something important happens.

People realize they are not alone.

Responders sometimes underestimate the significance of this presence because they focus on the practical tasks of the response. They measure success by the number of homes inspected, supplies distributed, or cases processed.

These metrics are important.

But survivors often remember something else just as clearly.

They remember the moment someone arrived to help.

A responder who listened.

A team that brought resources.

A volunteer who treated them with dignity when their life felt completely disrupted.

These moments may seem small compared to the scale of the disaster.

Yet they can restore hope at a time when hope feels fragile.

SEEING THE LONG ARC OF RECOVERY

Another way responders reconnect with purpose is by remembering that disaster recovery unfolds over time.

The early response period often focuses on urgent needs—shelter, food, medical care, and immediate safety. During this stage, the destruction may still feel overwhelming.

But recovery does not end when the initial response concludes.

Months and years later, communities often rebuild in ways that reflect the collective effort of responders, local leaders, volunteers, and residents.

Homes are reconstructed.

Schools reopen.

Businesses return.

Neighborhoods slowly regain stability.

Responders who step back and look at the long arc of recovery sometimes realize that the work they contributed during the early days helped set this process in motion.

They were part of the beginning of something much larger than the immediate deployment.

THE MEANING OF SERVICE

For many responders, disaster work also connects with deeper values about service and responsibility.

Some people feel a strong civic commitment to supporting their communities. Others are motivated by spiritual or ethical beliefs about caring for neighbors in times of crisis.

These values often shape how responders interpret their experiences.

Even when the work includes difficult moments, the responder may still believe that standing with people during disaster is worthwhile.

This belief can sustain responders through periods of frustration or uncertainty.

It reminds them that the purpose of the work is not perfection.

The purpose is presence, compassion, and assistance during times when communities need it most.

HOLDING THE HARD AND THE GOOD TOGETHER

Disaster response includes both difficult and meaningful moments.

Responders witness loss, disruption, and grief. They also witness resilience, generosity, and courage.

Communities often support one another in remarkable ways after disaster. Neighbors help clear debris, volunteers organize supplies, and survivors encourage one another during the long process of rebuilding.

Responders are part of these stories.

Even when they encounter situations where help could not be provided immediately, they are still contributing to a larger effort to support recovery.

Holding both sides of the experience—the hard moments and the meaningful ones—allows responders to maintain a balanced view of the work.

The goal is not to deny the moral tension that sometimes arises.

The goal is to remember that the work also contains genuine moments of human connection and service.

RETURNING TO THE QUESTION

From time to time it can be helpful for responders to return to a simple question:

Why did I choose this work?

The answer to that question often reveals something important about the responder's identity and values.

Remembering those motivations can restore perspective when the work becomes difficult.

It reminds responders that their presence in disaster response is not accidental.

It is part of a larger commitment to helping communities endure and recover from crisis.

And that commitment continues to matter, even when the work is challenging.

FIELD REFLECTION

What first drew you into disaster response work?

How has that motivation shaped the way you approach deployments today?

TEAM CONVERSATION

During a training or team meeting, ask:

"What keeps you coming back to this work?"

The answers often reveal the shared purpose that connects responders across many different roles and organizations.

Chapter 11

Staying Human in the Work

Disaster response asks a great deal from the people who do it.

Responders work long hours in environments shaped by loss and uncertainty. They witness the aftermath of storms, fires, floods, and other crises that disrupt people's lives in profound ways. They listen to stories of fear, frustration, and grief while trying to help communities regain stability.

Over time, this work can shape the responder in powerful ways.

Many responders say that disaster work deepens their sense of compassion. Seeing how communities come together during difficult moments often reinforces their belief in human resilience and cooperation.

At the same time, repeated exposure to crisis can also test a responder's emotional endurance.

Without intentional care, responders may begin to feel worn down by the constant presence of suffering. They may become less patient with survivors, more skeptical about recovery systems, or less hopeful about the possibility of meaningful change.

These reactions are not unusual.

They often appear slowly, developing over many deployments rather than during a single response.

The challenge for responders is to remain engaged in the work while protecting the very qualities that made them effective in the first place.

In other words, responders must learn how to stay human in the work.

RECOGNIZING PERSONAL LIMITS

One important step toward staying human is recognizing that responders have limits.

Disaster response culture sometimes encourages people to push themselves beyond what is sustainable. Long hours, back-to-back deployments, and constant responsibility can become normal expectations in high-demand environments.

While dedication is admirable, responders also need time for rest and recovery.

Physical exhaustion often leads to emotional exhaustion. When responders operate without adequate rest, their ability to process difficult experiences becomes weaker.

Taking time away from the field is not a sign of reduced commitment.

It is a way of preserving the strength required to continue serving over the long term.

MAINTAINING CONNECTION OUTSIDE THE WORK

Responders also benefit from maintaining strong relationships outside the disaster response environment.

Family members, friends, and community connections provide a grounding influence that reminds responders of the broader context of life. These relationships create spaces where responders can step out of the intense atmosphere of disaster operations.

Talking with trusted people about the work can also help responders process experiences before they accumulate into deeper emotional strain.

Even when others cannot fully understand the technical aspects of disaster response, they can often provide perspective and support that responders need.

ENGAGING IN REFLECTIVE PRACTICES

Many experienced responders develop personal practices that help them reflect on their experiences.

Some people write about deployments in journals. Others spend time in quiet reflection after returning home from the field. Some talk regularly with mentors or trusted colleagues who understand the realities of disaster work.

These practices allow responders to process the emotional and moral dimensions of their work rather than pushing those experiences aside.

Reflection helps responders make sense of what they have witnessed and integrate those experiences into their understanding of the world.

PROTECTING COMPASSION

Compassion is one of the most valuable qualities responders bring to disaster work.

It allows responders to treat survivors with dignity even during chaotic and stressful situations. It motivates responders to continue serving despite difficult conditions.

But compassion also requires protection.

Responders who give emotional energy continuously without replenishing it may begin to experience compassion fatigue. They may feel numb, detached, or impatient when faced with situations that once inspired empathy.

Protecting compassion often means balancing engagement with recovery.

Time spent with family, physical activity, hobbies, spiritual practices, or simply periods of quiet rest can help restore emotional energy.

These activities are not distractions from the work.

They are part of sustaining the capacity to continue doing it.

LEARNING FROM EXPERIENCE

Responders who stay in the field for many years often develop a deeper perspective on disaster work.

They learn that no single deployment defines the entire mission. They see patterns across multiple disasters and begin to understand how recovery unfolds over time.

They also recognize that even experienced responders continue learning.

Each response reveals new challenges and new insights about how communities cope with crisis.

By approaching the work with humility and openness, responders transform difficult experiences into sources of wisdom.

REMEMBERING THE SHARED MISSION

Finally, staying human in the work requires remembering that disaster response is not carried by individuals alone.

Responders are part of a larger network of people committed to helping communities recover from crisis. Colleagues, volunteers, local leaders, and survivors themselves all contribute to the recovery process.

Recognizing this shared mission reduces the pressure responders sometimes place on themselves to solve every problem personally.

The work is collective.

No single responder can repair every loss created by disaster.

But together, responders contribute to something larger than any individual effort.

That shared purpose helps sustain people through the long and sometimes difficult journey of disaster response.

FIELD REFLECTION

What helps you recover emotionally after a difficult deployment?

Are there practices or routines that help you reconnect with yourself outside the work?

TEAM CONVERSATION

Ask your team this question:

"What helps you stay healthy and grounded while doing this work?"

Sharing these strategies can help responders support one another in maintaining long-term resilience.

Chapter 12

The Work Still Matters

By the time a responder has spent several years in disaster work, they begin to see the work differently.

In the early deployments, the focus is often on learning the systems—how response operations function, how teams coordinate, how resources are distributed, how recovery programs unfold. The work can feel fast-paced and intense, filled with new experiences and responsibilities.

Over time, responders begin to recognize deeper patterns.

They see how disasters disrupt lives not only in the immediate moment but across long stretches of time. They observe how recovery can take months or years. They see how some communities rebuild quickly while others struggle with long-term challenges.

They also notice something else.

They notice that the work they and their colleagues do continues to matter, even when it does not solve every problem.

One of the difficult truths about disaster response is that no response system can erase the loss created by catastrophe. Homes destroyed by storms cannot always be rebuilt immediately. Lives disrupted by fire, flood, or tornado take time to stabilize. Communities must move through complicated processes of recovery.

Responders know this reality.

They see the gaps between what people need and what systems can deliver in the early stages of response.

Yet the presence of responders still changes the experience of disaster for the people affected.

When responders arrive in a community after catastrophe, they bring more than equipment, supplies, or logistical coordination.

They bring a signal.

The signal is simple but powerful:

You are not facing this alone.

For survivors, that message can be profoundly important.

In the first days after a disaster, people often feel disoriented and uncertain about what comes next. They may not know how recovery will begin or whether help will reach them.

The arrival of responders communicates that the wider community has not forgotten them.

Someone has come to help.

This presence matters even when the work is imperfect.

Survivors often remember the individuals who stood with them during the earliest stages of recovery. They remember the responders who listened to their stories, helped them navigate resources, or simply treated them with dignity during a difficult time.

These interactions rarely appear in official reports.

But they shape how survivors experience the recovery process.

For responders who carry memories of moments where help could not be provided immediately, it can be easy to overlook these quieter forms of impact.

A responder may remember the conversation where they had to say no.

But the survivor may remember something different.

They may remember that someone took the time to listen.

They may remember being treated with respect during a moment when everything else felt uncertain.

They may remember that someone cared enough to show up.

These moments accumulate across the entire response system.

Emergency managers coordinating resources, volunteers distributing supplies, counselors offering emotional support, and community leaders organizing recovery efforts all contribute to a network of care.

Together, these efforts create the foundation for recovery.

Responders are part of that foundation.

Understanding this broader perspective can help responders carry the moral complexity of the work with greater balance.

Disaster response will always include difficult moments.

There will always be situations where resources are limited, where decisions are complicated, and where outcomes are not as complete as anyone would wish.

These realities do not negate the value of the work.

They are part of the environment in which the work takes place.

What responders bring into that environment is something essential.

They bring compassion.

They bring skill.

They bring a willingness to stand beside people who are experiencing some of the most difficult moments of their lives.

And they do so knowing that the work may not always produce immediate or perfect results.

This commitment reflects a deeper truth about disaster response.

The work is not about achieving flawless outcomes.

It is about accompanying communities through crisis and helping them move toward recovery.

When responders understand this, the moments that once felt incomplete can be placed within a larger narrative.

The responder did not fail to solve the disaster.

They participated in the collective effort to help a community begin moving forward.

CARRYING THE WORK FORWARD

As responders continue in their roles, they accumulate both experience and perspective.

They learn how to navigate the operational challenges of disaster response more effectively. They develop stronger relationships with colleagues across agencies and organizations. They become mentors for newer responders entering the field.

Perhaps most importantly, they learn how to carry the emotional and moral dimensions of the work with greater wisdom.

Instead of ignoring difficult moments, experienced responders acknowledge them. Instead of carrying those experiences alone, they share them within the responder community.

They understand that disaster work will always involve complexity.

And they also understand that the work remains meaningful despite that complexity.

THE WORK CONTINUES

Disasters will continue to occur.

Communities will continue to face storms, fires, floods, and other crises that disrupt lives and require coordinated response.

When those moments come, responders will again step forward.

They will organize resources, support survivors, and help communities begin the long process of recovery.

They will also bring with them everything they have learned from previous responses.

They will carry the lessons, the stories, the wisdom, and the compassion developed through years of service.

And when new responders join the work, they will pass along not only the technical knowledge required for disaster response but also the deeper understanding of what the work asks from the people who do it.

That understanding includes recognizing the moral weight of the work, caring for one another within responder teams, and remembering the purpose that connects all responders across different roles and organizations.

The work of disaster response is demanding.

But it also remains one of the most meaningful ways people can serve their communities.

And for the people whose lives are touched by that service, the presence of responders will always matter.

FINAL REFLECTION

Think about the moments in disaster work that have stayed with you over the years.

Some of those memories may involve difficult situations orunanswered questions.

Others may involve moments of connection, gratitude, or resilience.

All of these experiences formpart of the story of your work.

Together they reflect the reality that disaster response is not only about logistics and coordination.

It is also about people standing with one another in times of crisis.

And that work—imperfect, demanding, and deeply human—continues to matter.

Afterword

What the Work Asks of Us

If you have spent any time in disaster response, you already know something that most people outside the field rarely see.

This work changes the people who do it.

Responders arrive in communities during moments when life has been disrupted in ways that few people ever expect to experience. Homes are damaged or destroyed. Families are displaced. Entire neighborhoods may struggle to understand what the future will look like.

In those moments responders step into a space where human vulnerability is very visible.

They see people at their most uncertain and sometimes at their most courageous.

They hear stories of loss, fear, frustration, resilience, and determination. They help people navigate the first steps of recovery when everything still feels unstable.

Over time, these experiences leave their mark.

Responders accumulate memories that remain long after a particular deployment ends. Some of those memories are difficult. Others are unexpectedly meaningful.

Together they form the story of the work.

This book began with a simple observation: disaster response carries a moral dimension that is often unspoken.

Responders enter the field because they care about people. They believe communities deserve support during crisis. They want to reduce suffering and help others regain stability.

Yet the realities of disaster response mean that compassion sometimes encounters limits. Resources may be scarce. Recovery may move slowly. Situations arise where responders must make decisions that feel morally incomplete.

These moments can stay with the people who experience them.

They can raise questions about fairness, responsibility, and the limits of what disaster response systems can accomplish.

Naming these experiences as moral injury is not meant to discourage responders.

Instead, it is meant to acknowledge something honest about the work.

Disaster response places people close to the deepest disruptions of human life. It would be surprising if that experience left no impression at all.

Responders who feel the moral weight of the work are not failing.

They are noticing the human reality of the situations they encounter.

And that awareness is often one of the reasons they are effective responders in the first place.

The goal of this book has not been to remove the moral complexity of disaster work.

That complexity will always exist.

Instead, the goal has been to help responders recognize the experiences they carry, talk about them with one another, and remain connected to the purpose that first drew them into the work.

When responders do this together, something important happens.

The moments that once felt isolating become part of a shared story.

Colleagues recognize similar experiences in their own deployments. Teams learn how to support one another through difficult situations. The responder community becomes stronger because people are willing to speak honestly about the realities of the work.

Disaster response has always been collective work.

No single responder carries the mission alone.

The same is true for the emotional and moral dimensions of the work.

Responders do not need to carry those experiences alone either.

When people share their stories, reflect together, and support one another, the weight of the work becomes more manageable.

And the purpose of the work becomes clearer.

Because beneath all the complexity, disaster response remains rooted in a simple commitment.

When people experience catastrophe, someone will show up.

Responders show up when communities need help organizing resources and restoring safety.

They show up when survivors need someone to listen.

They show up when the path toward recovery feels uncertain.

They show up not because the work is easy or because the outcomes are always perfect.

They show up because presence matters.

That presence is often the first step toward recovery.

Long after responders leave a disaster zone, communities continue the work of rebuilding homes, restoring routines, and reclaiming a sense of normal life.

But many survivors remember the people who stood with them in those earliest days.

They remember the responders who treated them with dignity when everything felt fragile.

They remember the assurance that they were not alone.

This is the quiet legacy of disaster response.

Responders may not always see the full results of their work.

But the compassion they bring into moments of crisis leaves an imprint that continues long after the deployment ends.

For the responder community, the challenge is to continue doing this work while protecting the humanity that makes it meaningful.

That means caring for one another.

It means speaking honestly about the difficult moments as well as the meaningful ones.

It means remembering that the purpose of disaster response is not perfection.

It is presence.

The work asks a great deal from those who do it.

But it also reveals something remarkable about people.

Again and again, when catastrophe strikes, individuals and communities step forward to help one another.

Responders are part of that story.

And as long as disasters continue to occur—as they inevitably will—the work of showing up for others will continue to matter.

So will the people who choose to do it.

Appendix A

Recognizing Moral Injury in Disaster Response

Disaster response places people in situations where compassion, responsibility, and the limits of available resources meet in complex ways. Responders often witness suffering, make difficult decisions, and encounter moments where help cannot immediately reach everyone who needs it.

Most of the time responders move through these experiences with resilience and support from their teams. But sometimes certain moments from the field remain vivid or unresolved.

This appendix offers a simple guide to help responders recognize when the moral weight of the work may be affecting them or someone on their team.

The goal is not to diagnose a problem, but to encourage awareness and conversation.

Recognizing the signs early can help responders process experiences in healthy ways and continue serving communities effectively.

Appendix A

SIGNS YOU MAY BE CARRYING MORAL INJURY

Responders who are experiencing moral injury often notice subtle changes in how they think about the work.

You may find yourself:

- Frequently thinking about a specific moment from a deployment
- Replaying conversations with survivors in your mind
- Wondering whether more could have been done in a difficult situation
- Feeling responsible for outcomes that were beyond your control

You may also notice emotional responses that feel unfamiliar or stronger than expected.

These can include:

- A quiet sense of guilt about something that happened during the response
- Frustration with response systems or procedures
- Sadness about the suffering you witnessed
- A lingering sense that something about the situation felt unfair

Sometimes the changes appear in how you relate to the work itself.

You may notice:

- Less enthusiasm about deploying again
- Feeling emotionally distant from survivors during new responses
- Questioning whether the work is making a meaningful difference

- A sense of fatigue that feels deeper than ordinary tiredness

Experiencing one or more of these reactions does not necessarily mean something is wrong.

In many cases, these responses simply indicate that you were deeply engaged with the human reality of the disaster.

Recognizing them early allows you to process the experience rather than carrying it alone.

SIGNS A COLLEAGUE MAY BE CARRYING MORAL INJURY

Responders often notice changes in colleagues before those individuals recognize the changes themselves.

You may observe that a teammate:

- Becomes unusually quiet after a difficult deployment
- Withdraws from conversations about the response
- Expresses frustration or cynicism about the work
- Avoids situations that previously felt comfortable

Some colleagues may talk about certain moments repeatedly, especially interactions with survivors that felt unresolved.

Others may say very little but appear emotionally distant from the work.

When you notice these changes, it does not mean you must solve the problem.

Often the most helpful step is simply reaching out.

A brief conversation such as "How are you doing after that response?" can create space for someone to share what they are carrying.

QUESTIONS FOR PERSONAL REFLECTION

Responders sometimes benefit from asking themselves a few simple questions after returning from the field.

You might reflect on:

- What moment from this deployment stayed with me the most?
- Was there a situation where the limits of the response system felt difficult?
- Is there anything from the deployment that I have not talked about yet?

Writing or talking about these reflections can help place the experience into a larger narrative rather than leaving it unresolved.

QUESTIONS TEAMS CAN ASK AFTER A DEPLOYMENT

Teams can also help one another by creating space for short conversations after difficult responses.

Some helpful questions include:

- What part of this response affected you the most?
- Was there a moment that felt morally difficult?
- What did you see during this response that reminded you why the work matters?

These conversations do not need to be long or formal.

Often ten or fifteen minutes of honest reflection can prevent responders from leaving the deployment with experiences that feel unfinished.

WHEN ADDITIONAL SUPPORT MAY HELP

Most responders process the moral weight of disaster work through conversation, reflection, and team support.

However, there may be times when additional support would be helpful.

Consider reaching out to a supervisor, peer support coordinator, counselor, or spiritual care provider if you notice:

- Persistent distress related to a specific deployment
- Difficulty sleeping or concentrating because of memories from the field
- Strong feelings of guilt or responsibility that do not ease with time
- A growing sense of emotional exhaustion or detachment from the work

Seeking support is not a sign of weakness.

It is one way responders protect their ability to continue serving communities in the long term.

A FINAL REMINDER

Disaster response places people close to the most difficult moments in the lives of others.

Responders who notice the moral weight of those moments are often the same people who care deeply about helping others recover.

Recognizing moral injury is not about labeling responders as damaged.

It is about acknowledging the human impact of meaningful work.

And when responders recognize that impact together, they strengthen the resilience of the entire responder community.

Appendix B

A Simple Team Debrief Guide for Disaster Response Leaders

Disaster response work moves quickly.

During deployments, teams focus on urgent tasks—coordinating resources, supporting survivors, communicating with partner organizations, and addressing immediate needs in the community. The pace of the work often leaves little time for reflection in the moment.

When the response operation slows or concludes, however, it can be helpful for teams to take a short period of time to reflect together on the experience.

These conversations do not need to be long or formal. In fact, brief and simple discussions are often the most effective. The goal is not to analyze every operational detail of the response. Instead, the purpose is to create space where responders can acknowledge the human dimension of the work and support one another as they transition out of the deployment.

This appendix offers a simple structure that team leaders can use for a short debrief conversation.

The conversation can take place at the end of a deployment, at the conclusion of a long operational period, or during a team meeting after responders return home.

Most teams find that 15–20 minutes is sufficient.

STEP 1: SET THE TONE

The team leader begins by acknowledging that disaster work can affect responders in different ways.

A simple introduction might sound like this:

"Before we wrap up, I'd like to spend a few minutes reflecting on this response together. We've all seen and experienced a lot during the past few days. This is just a chance to talk about anything that stood out to us."

The leader should emphasize that participation is voluntary and that responders are free to share as much or as little as they feel comfortable.

The goal is to create a respectful and supportive environment.

STEP 2: WHAT DID WE SEE?

The first question invites responders to describe their experiences during the response.

Ask:

"What is one thing you saw or experienced during this response that stands out to you?"

Responders may mention interactions with survivors, scenes from the disaster area, or moments that captured the emotional impact of the event.

This question helps team members begin reflecting on the response without immediately focusing on difficult experiences.

STEP 3: WHAT WAS HARD?

The second question acknowledges that disaster response often includes challenging moments.

Ask:

"Was there a moment during the response that felt especially difficult?"

Responders may describe situations where resources were limited, conversations with distressed survivors, or decisions that required balancing competing needs.

It is important for the team leader to listen without attempting to immediately solve or reinterpret the experience. Simply acknowledging that the moment was difficult can be helpful.

STEP 4: WHAT MATTERED?

The third question shifts the conversation toward meaning and purpose.

Ask:

"What moment during this response reminded you why this work matters?"

Responders often recall moments when a survivor expressed gratitude, when the team worked together effectively, or when a small action made a visible difference for someone in need.

These reflections help balance the difficult moments with the meaningful ones.

STEP 5: WHAT DO WE CARRY FORWARD?

The final question helps responders transition out of the deployment.

Ask:

"What is one thing you will carry forward from this experience?"

Responses may include lessons learned, appreciation for colleagues, or renewed commitment to the mission of disaster response.

This final step allows the team to recognize the value of the work they have done together.

THE LEADER'S ROLE

During this conversation, the leader's role is primarily to listen and guide the discussion.

Leaders should avoid turning the conversation into a detailed operational review. That type of evaluation often occurs in separate after-action meetings.

The purpose of this conversation is to acknowledge the personal and moral dimensions of the work.

Leaders can model openness by sharing a brief reflection of their own, but they should avoid dominating the conversation.

Creating space for team members to speak is more important than offering lengthy commentary.

WHEN THE CONVERSATION ENDS

When the discussion concludes, the leader can thank the team for their work and acknowledge the importance of what they accomplished together.

A closing statement might sound like this:

"Thank you for the work you've done during this response. What we've seen here matters, and the support we provided will help this community move forward."

Even a short moment of shared reflection can help responders leave the deployment feeling connected to their team and the purpose of their work.

WHY THESE CONVERSATIONS MATTER

Responders often carry powerful experiences from the field.

When those experiences remain unspoken, they can sometimes feel unfinished or isolating. Short conversations like this one allow responders to acknowledge what they witnessed and recognize that others on the team experienced similar moments.

Over time, teams that practice this kind of reflection develop stronger trust and resilience.

Responders learn that they can support one another not only in completing the operational tasks of disaster response but also in carrying the human weight of the work.

And that shared understanding helps ensure that no responder has to carry the difficult parts of the work alone.

Acknowledgments

This book grows out of years spent alongside people who respond when disaster strikes.

No one learns disaster work alone. Everything in these pages has been shaped by the experience, wisdom, and generosity of colleagues who have shared the field, the long hours, and the conversations that come afterward.

I am especially grateful to the emergency managers across the state of Iowa who carry the daily responsibility of preparing communities for the unexpected. Their steady leadership and commitment to public service form the backbone of disaster response long before a storm ever arrives.

I am thankful as well for the members of Iowa VOAD (Voluntary Organizations Active in Disaster), whose collaborative spirit reflects the best of what disaster response can be. The partnerships formed within VOAD demonstrate how organizations with different missions and traditions can work together for the sake of communities facing crisis.

My appreciation also extends to the dedicated professionals of the Iowa Behavioral Health Response Team, who recognize that disasters affect not only buildings and infrastructure but also the emotional and psychological wellbeing of survivors and responders alike. Their work reminds us that recovery is both practical and human.

For many years I have had the privilege of serving alongside volunteers and staff of the American Red Cross. Disaster response within the Red Cross is carried by people who quietly show up again and again when communities are hurting. Their compassion, professionalism, and endurance continue to inspire me.

I am also deeply grateful to the teams of Presbyterian Disaster Assistance, whose commitment to long-term recovery demonstrates what it means to accompany communities long after the immediate headlines have faded. Their work reflects a belief that rebuilding lives and neighborhoods requires patience, partnership, and hope.

Across all of these organizations—and many others not named here—I have encountered responders whose dedication to helping others in times of crisis reflects the very best of human character. The insights shared in this book are rooted in the experiences and conversations we have had together in the field, in training rooms, and in the quiet moments after deployments when responders reflect on what the work asks of us.

Finally, I am grateful to the families and communities who support responders in their work. Disaster response requires time, energy, and emotional commitment. The encouragement and understanding offered by loved ones make it possible for responders to continue serving others during difficult times.

To all who answer the call when disaster strikes, thank you for the work you do and for the humanity you bring into moments when it is needed most.

About the Author

Rev. Gregory C. Smith, PhD, is a retired Minister of Word and Sacrament in the Presbyterian Church (USA) with more than four decades of experience in pastoral ministry, disaster response, and spiritual care. He has spent much of his vocational life walking alongside individuals and communities in moments of profound disruption—natural disasters, personal crises, and the quiet aftermaths that follow.

Dr. Smith is a board member of the Iowa Disaster Human Resource Council and has been actively engaged in disaster spiritual care through partnerships with faith-based organizations, volunteer networks, and community response systems. His work focuses on the human and moral dimensions of disaster response, particularly the ways responders carry—and are shapedby—the weight of what they witness and what is asked of them.

A prolific author, Dr. Smith has written extensively on moral injury, resilience, faith, and the lived experience of those who serve in difficult and often unseen roles. His books, many published by Wipf and Stock, explore the intersection of theology, ethics, and real-world service, offering both practical guidance and reflective depth.

In Staying Human in Disaster Work, he brings together years of field experience, pastoral insight, and sustained reflection to offer responders a way to understand and endure the moral weight of their work—without losing themselves in the process.

Dr. Smith lives in the Midwest and continues to write, teach, and support those engaged in the work of care, response, and repair.

www.ingramcontent.com/pod-product-compliance
Lightning Source LLC
LaVergne TN
LVHW022112200926
848481LV00003B/1150
* 9 7 9 8 3 8 5 2 8 2 5 4 8 *